THE MOON AND OTHER FRUITS

Poems by
Frederick Livingston

Legacy Book Press LLC
Camanche, Iowa

For my grandmother
Anna Mae

May I carry burning words
on your torch

Contents

Praise for
The Moon and Other Fruits

"The poems, often rooted in a specific place indicated in their subtitles, take readers on a journey of exploration and reflection on the beauty and strength of life-cycles, on the flow of energy from rain and sunlight, into fruit, into us. A wise man is able to comprehend the secrets of life and share this knowledge with others. Here, 'enlightenment' means not some grandiose achievement, but understanding the flow of "waves within tides within lifetimes." It is good for us to read this inspired and inspirational verse... Highly recommended!"

—Dr. Maja Trochimczyk, President of California State Poetry Society, President of Moonrise Press, author

"Edward Abbey's famous advice to young people was: 'Flee to the wilderness! The one within, if you can find it.' Frederick Livingston has fled into the wilderness—both of the world and his own uncharted soul—and returned bearing gifts.

With astounding wordcraft and an unceasing sense of wonder, these poems take us on a journey that spans the planet, and the heart. If you've ever sat on a mountaintop, aching with joy and a desire that you can't quite put your finger on, these poems are for you. If you've ever stared at the moon and felt tears welling up in your eyes, these poems are for you. This is a book to put in your backpack, or keep under your pillow. These are poems to devour slowly, on a train heading into new and mysterious lands.

—Wess Mongo Jolley, author and editor

"From the garden to Kentucky, kitchen to orchard to Africa, Japan to forest trail, follow Frederick Livingston in "The Moon and Other Fruits" as he travels and honors the moment with deep attention to what's around him. In these well-considered lines he offers us what has grown and ripened between his well-tuned senses and the world... Take the hint to slow down and read these poems aloud. Listen and you'll be drawn in, asked to take part, and come out better for the journey.

The coherent love of synched sounds and related themes ties together the variety of density and light—like walking through forest, into meadow, and back—in ways that can keep contemplation and delight alive as you go."
                    —Don Freas, poet, designer/craftsman, sculptor

Awake to delight   then hunger
wander until you find a higher light

ONE

last night
I dreamed the Earth
was spinning
and awoke to illusions
of stillness

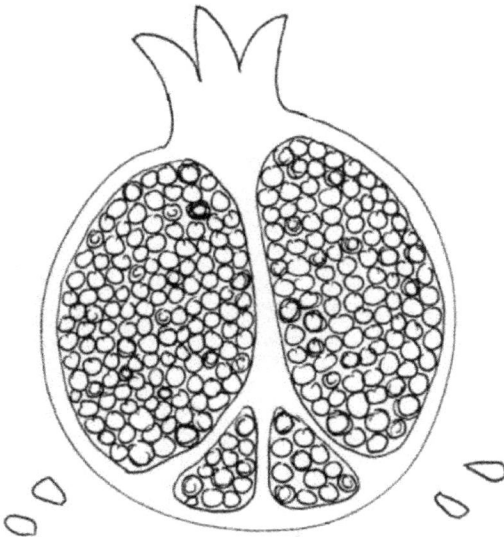

Gnat Creek
Oregon

This is no
        imperceptible wind showing its course
        in shifting smoke rising
        from our fire

No   this is
        plunge into river bringing mountains
        down to show us
        what cold is

This is no
        opalescent dew collecting on
        artist conk underbellies

No   this is
        fistfuls of bright huckleberries
        ornamenting the understory

This is no
        subtle poem

No   this is
        waking up in your arms

Praying
Sinkyone Wilderness, California

hours from uneven gravel

      we gather our fragrant things

      toothpaste, grapefruit peel, next breakfast

before laying under stars

dangling beyond reach

      we sling sack through high branches

      not because we've seen bears today

but because we believe

Present
Mendocino, California

three blue jays
take flight from limb
of red alder
just as my eyes
alight on them

let me never say
I made up a poem
but   if I listen
I might catch a few
and write them down

before they elope
with the boundless sky

Cape Town Book Lounge
South Africa

standing before the poetry shelf
overflowing with finding
      having and losing
it occurs to me
I've never had
an original thought

      in my life
her "you"
flows into
their "you"
and you flow
through me

when I stepped outside
a raincloud consoled me
     I know
     what it feels like
     to fall
     into a million pieces

originality no longer
concerns me
who would accuse
one raindrop
of plagiarizing heartbreak
     or laughter?

Do Stones Have Souls?
Dungeness Spit, Washington

if not
what is
it that
leaves them

when I lift one
from beach rubble
to gather dust
on my windowsill?

plum glass streaked
with green lightning
ember and ocean
tiger striations

spoke such particular
wordless vibrance
then faded
unremarkably grey

what if we see
in stones
the soul
of a place

scaled to senses
of hand heft
tongue salt
wet sunlit brilliance

nerve of living
Earth aching
for music
of touch?

these days I
only hold the stone
a moment
no pocket could carry

home
weigh the discrete
gravity of one
consider how

moon-washed tides
and sun-stirred wind
conspired to place it
precisely

here
in the hand
of an equal
miracle

Chainsaw Haiku
Willamette Forest, Oregon

walking down the trail
an obstacle: fallen tree
torn by winter storms

what rare clarity
to hold the correct tool in
this very moment

touch bark   soft with time
smell decomposing odors
read with great care first

glance of inert hulk
splinters into subtle clues
of frozen motion

bundle of tensions
compression, slope, leans and binds
look up for dangers

snip limbs   clear debris
deconstruct complexity
chart your escape route

ground feet in firm earth
breathe   motor coughs, kicks alive
align blade and wood

silence buried deep
moment of pristine focus
forest falls away

truth revealed in
visible forces   cascade
of frail pink ribbons

withdraw the saw   pause
to watch the log respond with
subtle creaks   test your

estimates against
gravity's authority
stop at the heartwood

saw up from belly
for a clean snap   but not so
far the saw gets caught

in the final cut
feel ache of life spent reaching
sky   hundreds of years

eaten ring by ring
in these vast final moments
at last   crackling groan

stand back   cut motor
stump rises in its root wad
trunk lands   sighs and rolls

fresh stillness settles
insight manifests   the path
now clear   beckons you

Migration
Mendocino, California

every scoop of pelicans I see
in blue skies between rains
      seems to be flying south

imagine explaining to them
our borders

the pelicans scatter
meander and gather
     no ghosts at their heels

where will all this
unbelonging go?

Forest Koan

Olympic National Forest, Washington

In old growth,
are shades of green
or names of the infinite One
more abundant?

Hemlock Alder Redcedar
Huckle Thimble Elderberry Salal
Devil's Club Witch's Hair Liverwort
Bracken Sword Licorice Fern
Vanilla Leaf Cleaver Wild Ginger
Pseudotsuga Urtica Mahonia

Unknowable diluted through enumeration:
sun-shard slips through canopy
to illuminate finite, decaying
cedar sheaves.

If I Were a Spider
Portland, Oregon

I would
hold you
so tight
I could
keep you

from falling
a part
of me
believes I
have enough

arms to
catch you
as dew
catches rainbows
on webs

I mean
the kind
of prism
that sets
us free

Rainbows Dreaming
Snoqualmie Pass, Washington

Now I know
the blankness of snow
is only rainbows dreaming,

teaming with streaks of red paintbrush
little lanterns of columbine
tiger lilies prowl the scree slope

yellow asters multiply the sun
the hungry green of spring leaves
purple-blue lupine flooding the valley.

Who would ever know
these slopes were covered in snow
one mere moon ago?

What else have I not seen
and called "empty" in my ignorance?
What dreams within me may erupt

from thawing soil,
simply waiting for ripe moments
to answer the generosity of sunlight?

RIPE

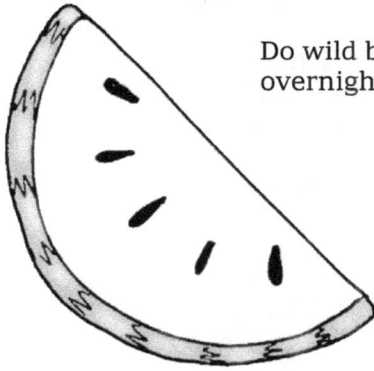

Do wild blueberries ripen
overnight as they dream?

crush one dewy
with cold dawn
on your tongue

and you
tell me

Mango Sunrise
Mora, Costa Rica

of things not confined to lines
        allow me to speak in rings
                concentric
                    electric
sun escapes day
        with agony of light
dusk blooms clues
        of your violet dress
for one
        slowly spoken glowing moment

gone before mangos fell
        or   mangos wept
                after you left
green at first
        then melt to wine
            green with thirst
        these arms of mine
worst of all
            is each one
gutter plucked

from crinkling clutter
        reveals rot riddled
        softness   squirming
turning over
        wonder cuts disgust
            this crisp instant asking
        who are you?
to refuse trading shoes with worms
           and come alive
into your own globe

of cloying glee   drink
sun slinks streaks
                 and shrieks of delight
night bargains dark heartbreak
          for dawn promises
yet every sunset   we sowed
               in loamy horizons
brought salvation
          beyond our most
                    insatiable salivations

sanguine saccharine skin signaling
          peel me
                   and feel the meal of me
cling to teeth in strings
                   plucked
ripe fruit of night falls
sun calls "I'll never leave you"
          then disappears from view
                   yet soon true
                        in hues forever new

Papaya
Mora, Costa Rica

sweat notes
sung low on sun glow
insipid flesh
blushes luscious

dusk after
brush against
unnecessary defenses
all walls dissolve

in watercolor language
beyond one
tongue's control
riches beyond conquest

too immense to carry
given lightly
ripe fruit fallen
is never stolen

aroma intoxicating
as freedom
silently suffusing
generous and irresistible

as sunset's invitation
to night
taste awaits
a moist awakening

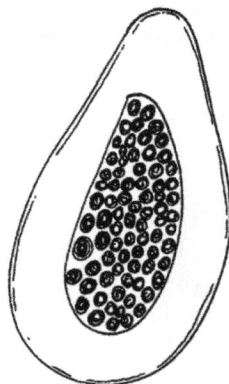

Fig
Mora, Costa Rica

like you
        I am no
true fruit
        succulent
at inflection point
        of senescence

but an inflorescence
        of sweet
swelling dreams
        encircling a buzzing
stinging
        winged being

except you
        know precisely
when to bloom
        for all those
who need
        and are needed
by you

Treasure Grove
Leaving Mora, Costa Rica

we dug love
           notes from stubborn earth
making holes in the grass
shovel struck glass
        bottle buried five Julys ago
           shattered to jagged shards
April reached in
        imbalance of curiosity and caution

cut her finger
a little
        blood
           read
           each folded letter
surreptitiously
        as if the lovers who wrote them
           might see me

syrup dripping
        from trees
        orange orbs half-hidden in green
        by overeager Easter bunny
laugh at my basket
        inadequate   to hold
    the sweet feast
        beneath my feet

I peeled them
        with my teeth
           sucked the sun
                warmed nectar
        until spilling
and somehow
more spacious
        than before

leaving what I could
                not carry
      to the wasps
             squirrels
             and all the other creatures
making their presence known
        only by the holes
             they leave

beside the broken bottle
        I will plant a citrus tree
        of unknown variety
            found in an
                  abandoned nursery
citrus reveals itself
        in sharp scent
        and thorns

but I am content
not to know
        whether it will grow
             sweet lemons
        or mandarin limes
        after I'm gone
            (too soon
            it will be June)

because I too have buried love
        in this fertile dirt
and it has borne fruit
        so far beyond
            what humble hunger musters
I no longer wish
        to trouble trees
            with all my foolish pleas

Desert Fruit
Serengeti, Tanzania

maybe once
this savannah was loud
with fierce beasts baring fangs

now, however, wind hushes
us through leafless thorn brush
sun runaways   we hunch

under thin acacia shade   conspicuous
citrus lips spit seeds on salt-stained earth
without worry they'd dare sprout

where water is dug   among
vulture feather and cattle dung
deep down the gorge

Maasai mother emerges
plaid swaddled infant in arms
and two twins in tow

sit in full sun   to watch
us dust-washed in said sad shade
unwrapping without appetite

white boxes
          yellow fruit
                    orange roots

we assume to be new, until
mother pulls camera phone from robe
to capture us

offering orange halves to her twins
tongue-tip to something fleeting
out of place and sharp as ice

Peach Season
Njombe, Tanzania

Before the juice dripping from her lips
became effervescent with laughter,
a teacher took his discipline whip
to lash a basket of peaches to his motorcycle.

Before boughs bent heavy
with sticky children,
a brother uncurled his sister's fingers from her broom
to make room for her pencil.

Before sour green buds were gnawed
by impatient toddlers, goats and worms
a mother sowed tree seeds
to grow school fees.

Before the verdant world awoke
from rain dreams,
little pink fools bloomed
in the bone dry, blue sky.

Lemon Season
Leaving Njombe, Tanzania

low breeze blows lemon leaves
dreaming sideways through time
I mistook these little green things for limes
rains arrived on time a year ago

    today

branches sway
unburdened by fruit I promised
to squeeze into open-fire pies
sunflower humus for your blender
if we slipped into next year

    yesterday

the hole beside my courtyard is filled
(God willing) by poles for wires
known to be live
I saw a crow dive too near
"whoosh-bzapt-thump!"
power of rivers separating us
brought inside
we'd live in light
though endless night
devouring all the green things
spring brings

    tomorrow

I'll walk past the tree
full of unripe lemon-limes
one last time
wondering   if in a year
I'll still taste sweet sour
delicious unease
of a new world becoming old
and an old world becoming new

Kumquat Season
Hazochu, Japan

when our lips
become unbearably   citric
we collapse   on spring-loaded floor

for a moment of electric hesitation
my blue eyes   meet   brown eyes
I caught this morning

as yoga sensei instructed us
to interlace   our toes
and "roll upu shimasu"   our spines

tingle when she enters
intersection illuminated by red-yellow
traffic pulse and white late-for-dinner car beams

her crooked smile   flashes
at my equivocal levitation
on trampoline beneath kinkan tree

lip-numbing fruit colored hair
and the garden gnomes stare at her   ankles
as she slips off her

shoes   we battle gravity
pluck dangling gold orbs
spit seeds or crunch

abruptly   dusk's door slams shut
I precipitate from dark sky
back to trampoline

still my hands are shaky
shaping fate
from the raw clay of dreams

Honey

With those who wonder
"what difference can one make?"
I will plant flowers

and when the buds bloom,
watch the little buzzing bee
whose life is made here

in the few hours
she has to gather all the
sweetness she will know.

Without faith enough
to plant my seeds in winter
there would be no bee.

Trees see us this way:
hurrying from place to place.
They hang fruit on limbs

to ask: "why not rest
a moment in my shade and
taste your precious breath?"

The bee takes my gift
to make honey. Flowers receive
the bee and make fruit.

Eat the fruit until
your fingers are sticky and
your belly is full.

"What gifts will you share?"
is the work of this world and
the meaning of joy.

Although industry
has filled our hands with pride,
always remember:

only by grace of
another's hope do we know
the nectar of breath.

Pear Blossom
Mendocino, California

this tree could be dead
or dreaming

dark gnarled bark
ringed in rows
of holes where
long-flown birds
searched for worms
in depths of winter

until sudden flush
of blooms consume
lichen-crusted branches
with white five-petal
promises of summer
swollen eat-me sweets

well before
glee-green leaves
greet sun
spun into sugar
proving dreams
precede the means

where is fear
of late-season frost
shattering this frail unfurling?
where are the rations
siloed inside against
lingering winter?

here instead is
chirping of birds returning
daffodils laughing
at the tree's feet
and a question
whispered low on cold breeze:

what would the world look like
if all of us had such courage
to offer our most tender selves
not only when spring is certain
but when we can no longer bear
our hunger for a more fruitful Earth?

HUN GRY

when jar escapes

your grasp,

shatters on the

kitchen floor

where does its

emptiness go?

Cholera Season
Njombe, Tanzania

rain-shaken mangos make thunder
rolling down aluminum rooves
mud craters become   amoeba breeding pools

humbling drumming flooding crowded room
doctor gasps wet air   shouts louder
rain danger warnings few believe

roofs were built by strangers
drowning under dry lectures no
they were made by lovers   intoxicated

with rain song we awoke new
immodestly verdant world   washed
last year's dust   whispers

of cholera   soon toothless
stumbling uncle   breath stale
sweet bamboo wine

dry earth cracks   green mangoes
open   roofs leak sunlight
fever dreaming   seasonal creatures

brewed moonshine truths   eagerly
devoured   last harvest
mama planted each seed

delicately   as if into mouth
of her back-borne infant   who could bear
imagine rains forsake her

fertile intentions   but sometimes we feed
insects and birds instead of loved ones
awaiting late rains

count   each   grain
eat or sow   believe in hunger
or believe in love   again

Snake Season
Klein Karoo, South Africa

Would you
       kiss me
under this acacia karoo
       if you knew
the mistletoe dangling
       from its veins will soon
suck its sweet sap dry
       and it will die?
Is this feeling
       true thirst   or
will tomorrow
       be worse?

Some count the drought
       from when the river ferns
withered
       or remember
the last time
       birds sang
storm songs
       others say it began
when we swam in
       exhaustible abundance
unable to sleep
       for the cacophony

of frogs
       rejoicing in the reservoir.
The damp soil
       held its fragrance
for days
       the way you remained
in my arms
       long after
our urgent embrace
       in the rain
wasn't final
       at the time.

We were bound to hope
        blood-red succulents
rooted
        in ochre stones
would you
        measure our distance
since
        in scents forgotten
in empty arm spans   or
        in crumbs
left clumsily
        in the kitchen?

We anticipated mice
        but not
the snakes
        that followed.

Evergreen
For Robert
Njombe, Tanzania

sunflower bursts endure
                    no winter
wither under
eucalyptus   fragrant
soil poison
throat medicine
crow homes
alive with cackling
numb
subtleties of form
wooden bones below
                    resewn
beehive box
fruit crate
              child coffin
              borne on mourning shoulders
last red petal
        in the valley
given
to winter wind

still

warm mornings
glistening dreams persist
green leaves breathe steam
hot afterbirth of dawn
                    spills
                    over jeweled meadow

Melting

For Anna Mae
Olympia, Washington

I heard you drained five liters of fluid
a week. Where does it come from,

I wonder?

Will I one day, be like ice cream too?
The last time I landed in your state

my eyes almost escaped their sockets
the pressure was so high.

I wonder

what kept them inside? We both know
it can't be merely flesh or churches

would serve sandwiches instead of sermons
better yet, ice cream, to keep us alive.

I wonder

which is worse: installing a faucet
in your body or realizing

you have no other way
to relieve pressure pooling in your legs.

But I wonder

who would want to be solid forever?
who can say it isn't better to run

down sticky chins, land in
sweet blooms beneath my grandchild's feet?

Inner Winter
Olympia, Washington

when your sunlight slipped
through cracks
in my clouds

I began to bristle and itch
wearing so many coats
while I was busy enduring winter

as a child
being fitted for a pirate costume
at the community theatre

I was told
I was a "winter"
meaning suited to blues

she was my intimate companion
far before you
and I

guard her jealously
from anyone whose footprints
might disturb our perfect snow

I've called her cold
but found no warmth
under all the fibers in my nest

I called her fatigue
but when I awoke
the ground was still frozen

I called her hunger
and ate until fear
leaked from my ears

I called her malaise
and filled days with anything
to keep my mind away

I learned how to survive
by gnawing
the skin of trees

how to burrow deep
within myself
in search of dreams

to turn chattering bones
into the hum of spring
but fear I've become

so familiar with winter
I've mistaken acorns for snow
because I am not

one season alone   no
winter is a season
from which I will grow

Grain Robbers
Mendocino, California

These little round birds
nibble fastidiously
at what appears bare

How many morsels
do I step on each day with
gaze so far from soil?

Cheery jesters now
but when summer ripens grain
I'll see them as thieves

Just as the slugs slurp
my lettuce and the gophers
disappear my leeks

I wonder to whom
shall I take my case, or is
my sweat all in vain?

Watching the birds hop
without a feather of guilt
I know there's no hope

for in the bird's law
the greatest crime would be to
waste a single grain

Desertification
Palm Springs, California

Dear   basking skink, house plant
        wall to wall windows,

I know how you crave sunlight
but the sweltering loneliness
of this Palm Springs family reunion
sees me swallow
IPAs abandoned in Airbnb refrigerators
        attempting to seep into the lawn
like the sprinklers responsible
for such an ecological anomaly
in the deserted   hours
between brunch and tea dance
I pray for green skin to receive this heat
spilling wasted on concrete streets
        when life seems impossible
it was healing to leave
the grid of boulevards
to find the city's namesake
laughing down boulders in palm shade
        savor the metaphor
enacted by following a stream
to its source
and remember   hope is no pool
        growing viscous with algae
        or evaporating to salt   no
something compels the invisible world
to spring from dry stones
inspiring oasis in its wake
whether or not it ever reaches the sea.

Sincerely,
        once-human raisin

Changing Names / Naming Change
Mendocino, California

after how many years
does "drought" erode
into expected weather?

and then what name
when the rains do return
startling the hard earth
the exhausted aquifers?

we'll sing to the deep wells
the quieted fire and clean sky
"winter" brittle in our mouths

holding vigil for rivers elders
insects lovers lost forever
when will grieving season begin?
what one word could walk

between delight of sun
hungry skin and unease
in receiving unseasonable gifts?

what of the breath we held
together as cold certainty melted
whispering "who burns this turn?"
when the broken record

record breaking
dips into new palettes
for our purple summers

cycles tighten
into teeth clenched
against unwavering anxiety
in which season do we open

our jaws lungs ears hearts
speak our fears
how it feels to be alive

on Earth still
blooming and unraveling
naming petals
as the wind claims them?

Space Between Us

Portland, Oregon

Looking up from
your sketch book
you ask
what am I
writing?
I am writing
space between us
as you give form
to ideas
with your pen

This space is
sometimes just like
a dry throat
full of water
waiting to swallow
and sometimes just
a dry throat

I don't know
how to draw
water from air
but I know
it is there

even if invisible
(but let's not
speak
of love)

Sometimes space expands
and I feel
tight as balloons
wondering about my
heart's elasticity or
are those
my branches
grasping sunlight?
as you can see

I sometimes try
to fill space
with words as
you might draw
a bridge only to find
you cannot walk
across

Sitting by the
river eating lunch
and sitting
by the river
eating lunch
is the difference
between light
and dark if one is in
love and one
is in fear

although the
same
breeze blows and
gulls still circle
for bread crumbs

Space can be
a river
between bodies
I could
measure each grain
gained and lost
from sedimentary
experience

and yet find
myself
no closer
to your shore

Some space is an
ocean
I
feel far away
staring at endless
horizons
yet

sometimes
when I crawl
along seafloors
(searching)
I cannot find
where I end
and you begin

There is no
space
between us
when I hold
you
in my
thoughts
the air
is your
skin

Tamarind Barbeque Sauce Recipe
Portland, Oregon

Maybe wash potatoes first
there's still tamarind in the pantry
you've felt this way before, remember:
- honey
- paprika
- salt, to taste

nothing goes to waste
not a half-used can of tomato paste
not love   (most famous among secret ingredients)

- Tickle kettle to song
- summon slumbering oven
- ease seeds from stringy flesh
- with scalding water

cayenne dash
          layering heat
some roots are worth roasting slowly
          coaxing sweetness from bitter earth

Excise unsightly potato eyes   from peel
you'll feel this way tomorrow still
cooking is looking
for the first time
     again and again at
- tongue-dance
- weight
- brightness
- and spice

spoon never stepping in the same sauce twice

Some mistakes are worth making:
overly sour tamarind
          softens bitter cinnamon
                    salt stokes pepper embers
                         harmonize with honey
you cannot pick just one
          and call it love

Oh! Brussels sprouts
languishing in the crisper
aching for language in the crisp air
on the park bench where your lips
      didn't taste hers
turn down sauce
      to simmer
loss arises
      from something
   worth having

- Halve the sprouts
- lay them out
- something else to think about

for now, dip in batter
      or leave bare
no need
to set a timer
you'll smell when they're tender

Aromatic alchemy: change is in the air
your only error
      was ever thinking
otherwise

- feast with your eyes
- eat with your fingers
- lick lingering flavors

like the chickens
      that tore your garden apart
your

- glowing
- growing
- beating   heart

RISING

while you sleep

I dream

of dawn rising

over us

in unimagined worlds

What to do with my Floral Bones
a living will

you should know
       before you go
       love me
i will grow   old
but also flowers in my garden

i do not strive to divide fleeting from beauty

of course
my eyes will slowly close
meanwhile i will practice tasting sunrise

my topmost hairs will wander
to my ears   and beyond
        hopefully
well after i lose
       my last strand of vanity
       or at least perfect my habit of hats

my habitat will be among my elders
trees to remind me where i stand
in a river of time
       always arriving
       present and departing
join me in the forest so we might whisper of silence

my ears will clog
       from a lifetime of sound
i may ask you to write things down
i hope by then i will have learned to listen
       to a beating heart
       from across the room

i may become aware of organs i never noticed before
as i cultivate pet aches
i may move more   slowly
       but with the twin desires of youth
         patience and purpose
more alive with stories than ever before
       a tree is mostly lifeless wood
         until it falls to the understory after all

becoming a banquet of new beginnings

you should know
        before i go
i will grow   mold
but also flowers from my bones

don't pretend i ever owned my soul
don't hide me from soil
        soaked in formaldehyde

rather huck and bury me
        beneath a huckleberry
so future generations can taste
my reincarnation   and see
it's not that i will become a skeleton

but that i always was one   underneath
these fluid robes you've come to know

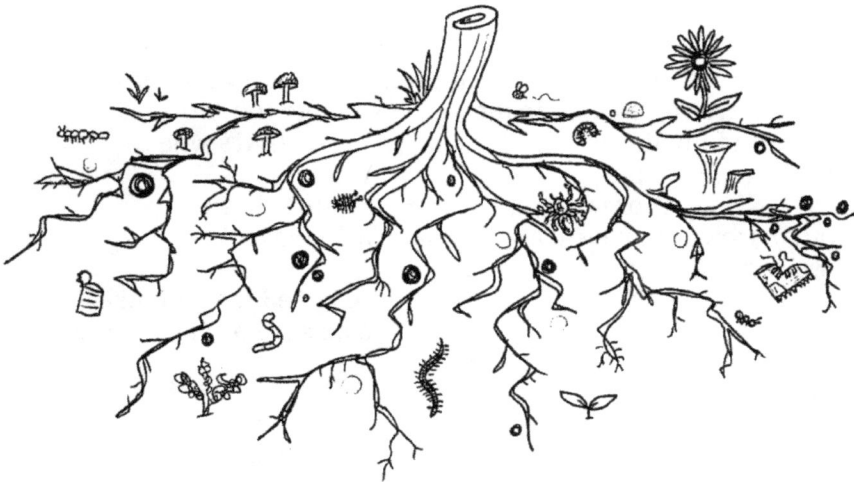

Study of Blood's Limits

Abstract

between arboretum and home   stopped at a red light
my father said he wished
for no regrets
        we know waiting   for green lights
    means clean hands
        full with a husband and two daughters
but never scarcity   of love
as his eyes watched the light change   I could see his stubble
flecked with sweat
        and soil   a new absence in memories
    and photographs
"it kills me" he said
        silence
broke through traffic sunlight through clouds
        road disappearing beneath us

Introduction

sister and I drove past warning signs
    "Biting Gnats are Bad"   "70mph Winds"
on the way to antelope island
at sunset we gathered stones
        to weight the corners of our tent
    but the walls still thrashed in the wind's jaws
I asked if we were going to die   she told me "no"
    and I believed her   that's what
family means to me
    more than the blood we didn't share
though growing up we were told how alike we look
dawn brought calm
        we tasted the salt lakes
        to be sure of their name

Methods

I dreamed
my father sat on a green couch   I stopped
in front of his address
    on a noisy street   crumpled the directions
into my pocket
    I walked in
without knocking
    told him who I was   how it all was

then turned around and never looked back

but really
my father was across the country
when he got a call from my mother
      for the first time
           "sit down   are you the man
      who gave a bit of himself to a yogurt cup
      nearly eighteen years ago?"
it took us that long to realize
his name had only ever been hidden
by a layer of paste on the donor form
he said he didn't know
                      until she showed him baby photos

if he took the news same as me
he sat on his bed   pondering grooves in the wall
      laid down in the grey afternoon light   felt the
earth spinning
for the first time
      woke to a dark sky
waited   a long time
      for the next day to begin

Results
day after Christmas   I have no memory
of ever being this nervous
      waiting   outside his address
as though eighteen years needed ten more minutes
            yes
eventually we walked through the gate overgrown with vines
saw two men
in the window   "sit down"
      warm over-brewed tea   dusting off old photo albums
when my father returns from the car he realizes
my two new sisters
         thought I was hiding in the trunk
"no
      here is a photo"
the older one always wanted an older brother
      the younger slowly
         falls over
           in her chair   I remember
      being this nervous before

midnight Kentucky thunderstorm   we arrive
        a new cousin runs to his mother   "you never told me
        Harry Potter was in our family!"
the Ukrainian exchange student says I look like Elvis
        people see what they want to see
next morning cousin continues open-mouth kissing
the family cat
        my new aunt discusses her plans
        to marry me to the exchange student
so humid your sweat never dries   lightning bugs
can smell it as you
                    chase them with jars

Phoenix bakes us   self-titled "G-ma" insists
        "show up old and you get weird presents"
sock monkeys the size of chimpanzees
        red for me and two green for my sisters
returning through airport security
        sticky children tug their parents' hands in envy
                took years convincing G-ma to stop
                sending us more monkeys in the mail
wearing Santa hats, Easter baskets, corresponding to holidays
we fell asleep across one another   soaring over purple
cactus groves

Discussion
dry season in Njombe
        every trip down dust roads worth your letters
                            and chocolate
    "sit down   maybe make a cup of tea"
                        I went down to the waterfall

55

             past the men washing motorcycles
"where do I begin?"
             night before I left Seattle   my fathers slept
in separate rooms
                         one of them must snore   I thought
"why is only death considered success
         and seventeen wonderful years together is failure
         because it ends?"
in two years   return to Seattle
                                              visit my fathers in
                                    separate houses
new families to add to my
                              story that doesn't end
is what living   *loving*
                                         means to me

Dandelion Coffee
"Chinchin puipui" farm, Japan

What unsettled me most
was not the ubiquity of bead curtains,
the awkward hand-drawn dragons
crawling across walls,

or the furry pink toilet seat.
It was the way the clock menagerie
chimed separate senses of time
scattered throughout the hour.

Cuckoo chirps, then Charlie Brown
Christmas jingles, later grandfather
clock bellows, on and on. Adrift in time,
I lay my roots in wandering soil.

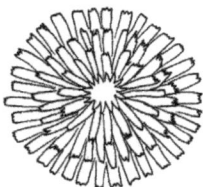

Laugh track wafts over empty playground
while child in idling van watches cartoons.
His mother and I pry our horihoris
(father stayed home getting stoned)

beside ragged rosettes, liberating dandelions
from earth carefully as if each was a rare
and precious jewel. I too feel like a weed
sometimes, agreeable to any bare ground

but feeling nowhere at home.
I wish someone would delight
in my common flowers, roast my roots,
savor my bitter flavors.

In Defense of Language

guttural thunder's hissing heave
between fricative wet salt smack

shape spoke skeletal scrape to thought
concrete fraught lingual knots

soul moaned for form
forgave name's erasure

ears wake howling stars ablaze
humming buzz from sunning moon

amniotic cerulean Eros
cackle snapping kindling twigs

vowels invertebrate slurp
all slime voluptuous ease

inured swoosh in lurid flumes
not cough snot glottal stops

consonant lovers of friction
afflicted with fictive kin

slug and skirmish emerges
fickle disparate urges

discord vocal or umbilical?
confine define redefine

coarse warp weft breath
ambulating flesh exhales *"wwhhyy?"*

wind swoons emerald ectoplasm
knife snarls horizon's gold throat

back towards known coasts
exposed bone roams homeward

all poems
are love poems

Starfish
Bellingham, Washington

There were signs my resolve was not absolute.
I bothered to wait in line to buy the wine, instead of walking out
like nothing mattered.
I followed the sidewalk down to the bay.
I even found a recycling can in someone's yard to dispose of the
empty bottle.

I took coins from my pocket
planted them on the train tracks that snake along
the rocky shoreline
waited for the train to erase them,
make them smooth and new again.

When rumbling subsided, I put the coins back in my pocket
stood in the tracks and waited
for the next train

for a long time.

Eventually the rails shiver like it might rain
or a prickling suspicion of lightning strike.
A shrill warning whistle emerges from fog,
mounting pounding heart undefined from world shaking.

I was sure to bring enough wine
to keep my thoughts from walking in straight lines
because I knew where they could lead
and found no rest in those dark places.
How I devoured whole chilies
to burn through the clouds for a moment.
I once ate a burrito the size of a new-born child
and still felt empty.

Time steadily swallows space for second chances
in that murky mind muck some sense of self
preservation fumbles with the controls
begging legs, sending dizzying signals
to step aside...

And I lingered
as if to dare the sky to open and
show me a power greater than miles of careening steel.

I watched myself step off the rails
well before the train reached me
left without an answer, only a riddle:
a hungry heavy enveloping "why?"
I walked down the creosote boards and rusted irons
across a weathered bridge,
stopped when something underneath caught my eye:
piles of purple starfish
in perfect repose on jagged rocks and barnacles
at the mercy of waves and vagaries of salt, water and sun
so serene and inexplicably...
beautiful.

My mind jumble found nothing
to explain this royal color.
What predators are they warning?
How could this attract a mate with no eyes?
Something bubbled up from below,
something beyond the architecture of my understanding
that shook my bones with haunting song.

I was bewildered, shivering, drunk and alive.
I walked home in silence,
crawled into bed and fell asleep.

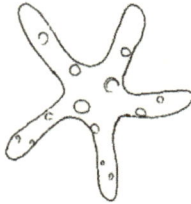

Years later, I work with young people
the same age I was at my lowest
and see how many feel alone in this unspoken experience,
a rite of passage in a land of eroding milestones.

So when a boy in the limbo of uncertain adulthood
tells me he is covered in hives, his bones ache
and he feels like jumping off that water tower over there,
I struggle with this intimacy of pain.
What should I tell him?

When I find a young woman curled under a fern
far from the trail, silent as stones…
What should I say? That everything will be okay?
I could never look them in the eye and pretend such certainty.

Should I tell them they will climb out of this hole
stronger than before,
recite the nobleness of suffering,
platitudes about the darkest hour before dawn?
Not when I know how meaningless tomorrow becomes when the
world stops spinning.

Should I tell them instead that they are right
to feel this way?
Maybe this is what it feels like to be born
into a shared spiritual crisis.
The Earth is burning
and your culture is pouring gas to stay warm
in the cold loneliness of its narcissism.

Or, can I take their hand, walk down to the train tracks
where starfish lounge
touch the spiny tenderness
and tell them to listen to that whisper
of the world beckoning…

Come into my arms sweet child
you do not know how beautiful you are.

There is a light glowing on your horizon
you can hide your eyes or turn your back
but it will be waiting for you.

Love has patience beyond your life
and when you are ready you will walk towards it.

You will not reach it tomorrow
or the next day,
you may even stumble backwards or sideways
but gradually you will feel its glow growing
with possibilities
that you might sleep tonight,
that you might wake,
not entirely whole
but maybe having found one more piece of yourself
scattered across the landscape of your dreaming:
in the tide pools swimming with tiny creatures
inviting us to kneel and imagine lives smaller
and briefer than our own,
in the irrefutable ocean that does not indulge
our notions of self-importance,
breathing time in endless, ephemeral waves.

So go-
The world aches to know you

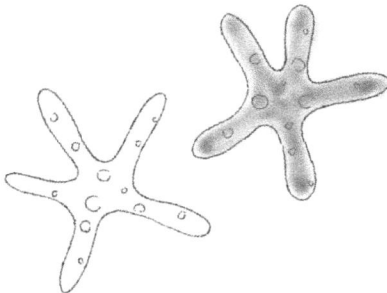

Abalone
Mendocino, California

when first we saw them
glistening like oil slicks

felt the smooth
sea-tumbled

not quite metallic
or crystalline

mysteries in our
wind numbed fingers

intuitively we knew
we must be the first

humans
to discover these

puzzle pieces strewn
across the grey shore

or else we would have
heard of them before

equally believable
as scales shed

by some shimmering
sea serpent

or as trinket shards
washed up

from an ancient
truck stop gift shop

no less alien
after hearing them called

"abalone"
conjured no silhouette

in shadow puppet theatre
of mind

returning after
whirling full circle

focus lifts to multitude
fragments of bone

broken stones
soft bodies in fragrant decay

at the ocean's swaying edge
at once

so intimately aquamarine
and distantly blue

all clues to a world full
of unknowable wholes

seen only in
visible scattered glimpses

why then is this feeling
so familiar and new?

because my world grew
as it has continued to do

ever since
I discovered you

Love Over Oceans
A proposal for extracurricular research
Costa Rica to the Netherlands

Abstract

Never underestimate the heartbreak of the big bang. Imagine a force capable of compelling an ecstasy of infinite singularity to scatter into a vast, cold, and dark universe.

Tangible

I want to live in a world with the environmental allowance for lovers to fly across the world to be with one another. I want learners to be able to voyage to the edge of their known universe so that they may be confronted with the bewildering landscape of human possibilities: within and without. I wish everyone the freedom to move until they know they always belonged.

Yet I know this is not the case. I am an anomaly in time and space. So I try to plant trees and compost my melon rinds and smile at strangers and look down at the world from little airplane windows to be moved by smallness: without and within.

Introduction

You say my journey lacks academic excuse. And this is probably true. Still, it is movement towards truth and a fuller expression of what my life can be, so I see no conflict in our goals. I would not miss your class if there was another way.

Conduction

Touching earth roots me to what is real and I can feel the joy of what may be without leaving the ground, my head in clouds.

It would be too harsh a separation to send my soul across an ocean before my body could reach those shores. We are learning what miraculous closeness is possible in distance,
yet the universe is not only expanding.
It pulls us closer too.

Methods

I will prepare nuts and dry fruit for fortitude. I once made the mistake of bringing salad through security and I had to convince the officer that it was not a liquid by eating it. I will spread peanut butter onto bread, because it only counts as liquid in a jar. Rubber snakes. Sporks. I have learned many lessons from loss. Where I am going is far. And cold. And dark. It is the universe, so I am bringing every sweater I own: exactly one.

I will rest best I can, although I have dreams overflowing even in day. I will hurtle across lines in the sand, to lands where clocks disagree with me. I will bring paper and tea for collecting thoughts. I will drink water and seek vegetables and emerge through winged cocoons newly enamored   with sunlight.

Discussion

So why did the universe decide to burst forth? Why shatter perfection into uncountable shards? Why carve trees into boats to chase the horizon? Why challenge the gravity calling us to Earth? Why leave paradise to burn candles and bundle in coats?

Because this is the only journey.

Rings

tell me if this rings true for you
we've seen mean seasons

like winter midnight in Delft
when you took your roommate outside
to show them snow

for the first time
or other days

you were a world away
like any words I said
less important than

"I love you"
but also lush abundance

like the humid evening
you cleared the gates of San Jose
hours before lockdown

lips soon sticky with mango
and birdsong

or the simple miracles we collected
watching ocean swallow the sun
and every shared breath

in these rhythms I read no erosion
ups and downs scrubbing sand from stones

I see rings where our cells grew
close and slowly
remembered as dark lines in our marrow

between soft and generous space
the spine supporting our pursuit of sky

I see growth
because we can turn the leaves we shed
into flowers

because there is more than enough
sunlight for two lifetimes

Light
Mendocino, California

sunbeam alone
        is a poem
but on this fallen log
        with you

everything is
        tongue tip
fingertip
        heartbeat

who was I?
        sweating brick
by brick
        over gilded cities

as if
        to impress
the heavens
        with my cleverness

as if
        to invent
anything
        as alive

as this urgent
        syrup
melting into
        our veins

warming
        pine-steeped air
Earth was made
        for breathing

Sky in Fall
Mendocino, California

what I forgot to tell you
after our first good rain
was how the sweet air
was heavy with insects
murmuring hallelujah

curtains of termites dizzy
with the newness of wings
spilled from a willow
nervous with yellow jackets
and frothing with aphids

like them, I must have
survived dry spells but
none of us dwelled in thirst
that day burning with awareness
suddenly blue and cloudless

MOON

hold

hearts with

open hands as

gravity holds her breath

halfway between fall and flight

Moon Sugar
Njombe, Tanzania

Sudden and thunderous here, darkness falls
    down a flight of stairs, spilling invisibility,
reminding us how slowly light is coming. Too long ago
    tar-filthy entrepreneur and his tar-filthy apprentice
planted a water wheel in the river, were seen

    dragging wires through the village like endless tails.
Postholes were dug like prayers, fulfilled
    by unwary ankles and mosquito brood.
Now moon has found her first competitor
    glowing at the end of a eucalyptus pole

dim as rumors of phones we will charge,
    light termites will mistake for moons
as we slap them into bowls to fry
    when air is electric with rain-smell and wings,
or a TV, if we dare to dream. Rain is heard

    before it is seen. Thirsty earth applause
roars loud as pop music from dry-season weddings.
    Before these flatulent subwoofers echoed
over hills, some remember radio. My neighbor remembers
    pounding feet and goat-skin drums.

Weeding beets, my students proclaim "too red" to eat
    one turns to me, "teacher, you are the color of teeth!
Teeth that bite everything!"
    What could I say? She was right.
I owe my bright teeth to the night sky.

    Brushing while counting stars, impatience melts
in whims of moonlight: her inky absence,
    her grin widening nightly until moon beams
make the world sweet and new again
    as a bar of forgotten chocolate, found miraculously

uneaten by rats. I dream of them baking cakes
    from all the avocados, chilies, soap, underwear
they've stolen while I sleep, over stubborn coals
    left smoldering on cold winter nights.
Streetlights grow on streets. Dirtlights illuminate nothing

like overfull moon dusting silver sugar everywhere, whispering
"I've-made-too-much-cake-won't-you-all-
    help-me-eat-some?" A forest of streetlights has enough
electricity to fry the moon like an egg, but some teeth ache
    for more sweetness in this new world without night.

Lunar New Year
Mora, Costa Rica

In this new moonless, cloudless season
stars emerge from black sky
seemingly   for the first time.

Below, city spills across the valley
as though a thief on the run stumbled
with a sack of gold and silver.

My lamp catches sapphires in the grass
and   leaning closer   I see
countless pin prick eyes
of tiny spiders I hadn't considered in day.

This is all to say:
your light finds its way into my world,
for to speak of beauty
is to feel you   walk beside me.

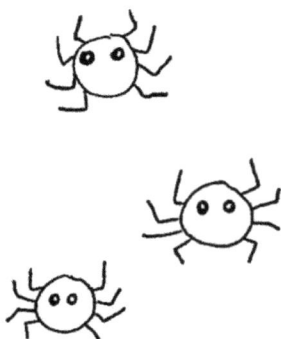

Our Eyes
Mora, Costa Rica

Although our eyes are a mere blink in time
I can see

we discovered love
before taming fire

because our heat is deeper than skin
I sleep in sweaters without you

we made love
before the wheel

because holding you
there is no place else to go

we spoke love
before any language

because our sounds are only flowers and frosting
on silence

we felt love
before gravity

because I know the pull
of being someone's moon

love arose
before atoms scattered to every corner of our cosmos

why else would they be
together to begin with?

long before first sight
the life behind your eyes replied to mine

and I see
what everything could be

Drip
Mendocino, California

I am watching
water gather
on the tip
of the faucet

across the room
gradually growing
finite as gravity
takes notice

a drip becomes
a drop
and when it falls
I catch your breath

in my mouth
fill my lungs
with you
until inspiration dips

into exhalation
and I am giving you
my life now
I am listening

to waves
discuss eternity
with jagged
black rock

and vanishing paths
of creatures
seeking
salty shore morsels

I have found
the bed
where the sun
lays down

where world ends
and ocean goes on
forever
is a place

I want
to be
with you
in this moment

the moon above
always changing
constant companion
so heavy with light

even seeds swell
in the spell
of her
undulations

first roots
then shoots
burst earth
leaves unravel

introspection of buds
petals beckon
a more beautiful world
wilting to eager seeds

for final leap
of wind blown
hope
I am walking

in our garden planted
in laughter
rain
strain

and sunlight
welcoming weeds
as guests
with lessons

love overgrowing entropy
the way leaves and light
and surf and cliffs
and skin and skin

bring each other alive
to what gifts
we were given
to give

I am seeing unnamed colors
and smelling flowers
of fruits
yet untasted

I am counting
widening rings
spinning around
and in revolutions

of the sun
curling into winter
and unfolding
with summer

the water drop
from the faucet
across the room
lands

in mute conclusion
perceptible only
in this silence
becoming

something
eternal again
although
every moment

arises
and passes
over time
I am filled

with
the love
you
are

Tide Riddle
Mendocino, California

Question:

if the tide is lured by the moon
why does it rise
twice
each day
if the moon
only circles us once?

Answer:

moonlight stirs the water it illuminates
into aching tongue-hanging
lapping against its shore

Earth too   is not immune
tugs the tether of its orbit if only
to be a moment closer   to her glow

but why does the sea
on Earth's moon-dark side   also rise
when Moon is at her furthest?

imagine tasting moonlight
then watching her slip behind Earth
how could that flavor   ever escape you?

as Earth leans moonward
the seafloor drops like a swallowed heart
and in these depths we see "rising"

and so   there is nowhere on Earth
you could go   where I
could ignore the pull of you

Midnight Noon
Ruaha, Tanzania

Moon threw shadows
heavy as bricks
through my window.
I awoke
to clattering dream shards
on the floor.
Sweeping off sleep dust
I went to the window
to investigate
this luminous commotion.

Cream spilled
through the open shutters
flooding my room
with light.
Worried I might drown
I crawled
out of the window
and into
an entirely
new world.

The thorn forest
beyond my door
was grey
as death
before.
Now
shyest acacia and
most resplendent flamboyant
dripped with
equal lunar luster.

Speckled leopards
and emerald sunbirds
emerged uncertain
to say
if this was night
or day.
I would have sworn
myself still asleep
if not for the dream pieces
glistening on my bedroom floor.

What more
could I thirst for?
I reached for the moon
but grasped only
the enchanted air.
Despair lurched first
but knowing glowed slowly.
I will never measure
from here to her
with fingers or feathers.

No
she is somewhere
numbers won't go.
Though, as my gaze drank
this deliciously silver
twilight, I saw
no matter how far away
her presence has
lit my world
with possibilities.

Constellation
Mendocino, California

I have seen many maybe-whales:
surf disturbed in a certain way
waking nerves alert and sky-wide
transfixed by the vague
suggestion of a creature
one fin in this world
and one fin outside

                                  subside in a breath
                                  as a wave slinks from shore
                                  pretending
                                  it didn't just throw
                                  all its passion
                                  at the Earth's feet

          as we rolled behind sight
          of the sun
          the sherbet-flooded sky drained
          and two lights became faintly visible
          above the horizon
          just as the other sunset-watcher
          we met last night
          predicted
          planets, he said,

                            here for a few nights
                            every eight hundred years
                            or so
                            or at least four hundred,
                            he retracted

but the difference felt
less burning
than where will they go
and why have they come all this way
to visit us now?
returning from your walk
along the cliffs
you reported seeing a string of lights
flow across the sky
and we observed
there must be at least a few people around here
who could afford a UFO

maybe even for the amusement
of confusion alone

                                I'd like to believe
                                I can pick a planet
                                out of a line of stars
                                but across such
                                inconsolable distance
                                who can be sure?

          I have heard a whale's tongue
          is as a big as an elephant
          and its heart is big
          as an automobile
          with veins large enough
          to swim through

                                I don't know if this is true
                                but I tend to believe so
                                simply because it is
                                a preferable world
                                to inhabit

then again
I've also heard people say
a star is bigger than a whale
but what use are such comparisons
to me?
they even say stars are made of fire
and flying through space
faster than a cormorant
swoops into fish-rich sea

          or is that a harbor seal swimming
          in the limits of my vision
          all motion blurs
          back into the swirl of maybe-everything
          from which we all emerge

my first
unmistakable whale
was different

                                there!
                                beyond those bird-thick cliffs
                                distant yet distinct
                                my heart leapt into the waves
                                with a spray like rain

as a child born in a city
I remained skeptical of constellations
the overlay of mythic figures
on what meager stars the light-full night offered
seemed fanciful at best:
seasick sailors imagining mermaids
from manatees

                    but the closer I get
                    to the sky
                    the clearer I see
                    we too are but two
                    points of light
                    adrift in darkness
                    given meaning
                    by our connections

      that is how my heart
      left my chest to pound against the waves
      when the whale precipitated
      from the brewing, brooding clouds of what-may-be
      suddenly a sea of frightful, lurking uncertainty
      became glass quiet and I saw
      firmament has not
      escaped me entirely

                    to feel your heat-loving fingers
                    in the coat pocket we share
                    an intimacy so far
                    from ambiguous sea monsters
                    or luminous intimations
                    of hidden moons
                    or the ungraspably vast chasms
                    of wordless matter
                    between us
                    and the things we claim
                    simply because we have
                    given them names

despite all of this
here you are beside me
and I have seen a whale
I have seen a planet
and I have known love
far brighter than them all

Darklessness
Portland, Oregon

I feel how night feels
moon. Do you diminish
me? No, you
give me
meaning.

I feel how bowl feels
empty. Are you my
hunger? No, you
are my
possibility.

I feel how soup feels
spoon. Disassemble me slowly?
Yes, bring me
to your
lips.

All Poems are Moon Poems
Mora, Costa Rica

Moon is a basket of clouds
swaddled in gloom
Moon is the only egg left in the nest
Moon is a balloon now
rising from clouds below
into clouds above

Moon is the eye
of one boundless dragon winking
swimming without stirring ripples
wakeless
never truly sleeping
half concealed even in fullness

Moon is a piece of Earth
lost in a distant collision
lingering at arm's length
ungraspable
Moon is too big to hold in the mind
Moon fits in the palm of one hand

Moon slips through mist
on the tip of a tongue
unspoken
Moon says everything
Moon is all the white in the sky tonight
floating unfurled of worldly burdens

circling a swirling Earth
          and
sitting on the stoop under Moon with you
tonight
my heart
my heart is the rising Moon

The Moon Rose
Joshua Tree, California

the moon rose
    slowly
bloomed

the moon petunia too
   soon bluebell
violet   and marigold

the mountain thorns
   adorn
slender twilight   stem

dawn roots
   deep
     in night

something more
   than an absence
     of light

Thanks to

The people of Alki, who made my sixth-grade television debut, "Ode to a Chair," possible. Especially Val.

The teachers who encouraged me to write,
whether or not I made any sense. Especially Mrs. Violette.

The Bellingham poetry community, who helped me feel what poetry could be. Nancy, Mike, and everyone.

The artists whose skills helped this book reach for what it could be. Especially Mongo and Anna.

My family for their ideas and nourishment.
And to everyone who has accompanied me in my journey:

Those who challenged me, expanded me, filled me with gifts to share with the rest of the world.

A WHIRLWIND UNFURLED CURLED FERNS WITHIN ONE FERTILE WORLD WHILE TWIRLING

10% of the royalties from this book will be donated to the Thurston County Food Bank. *Thurston County* because of my roots. *Food Bank* because poems should feed people, in both mind and body.

About the Author

Frederick Livingston grew from the southern tip of the Salish Sea in Olympia, Washington. Ecology, experiential education, and peace building have given him years in rural Tanzania, Costa Rican highlands, the American West and beyond. His writing has appeared in numerous literary magazines, scientific journals, and public spaces. This is his first collection of poetry.

Previous Publications

"Evergreen" – *Jeopardy Literary Magazine*, Issue #53 2017

"Moon Sugar" and "If I were a Spider" – *The Laurel Review, Fearsome Critters Journal*, 2018

"Gnat Creek" – *Garfield Lake Review*, Spring 2020

"Tamarind Barbeque Sauce" – *The Ear Literary Magazine*, Fall 2020

"What to do with my Floral Bones" – *Plants & Poetry Journal*, September 2020

"Mango Season" – *F3LL Magazine*, Summer 2021

"Pear Blossom" – *Bacopa Literary Review*, October 2021

"Love Over Oceans" – *Book of Matches Literary Journa*l Issue 4, January 2022

"Abalone", "Cape Town Book Lounge", "Honey", "Migration", and "Praying" – *Ginosko Literary Journal*, Issue 27 2022

"Constellation" – *Willows Weep Review*, Issue 23, December 2021

"Desert Fruit" and "Snake Season" – *Down in the Dirt Magazine* V.194 and *The Ice That Was* collection book, April 2022

"Present", "Sky in Fall", and "Starfish" (print). "Abalone" and "Constellation" (online reprints) – *Honeyguide, Field Guide Magazine*, Spring 2022

"Changing Names" – *Writers Resist*, March 2022

"Grain Robbers" – Torrey House Press, *In the Garden Chapbook*, April 2022

"The Moon Rose" and "Lemon Season" – *Impspired, Volume 8 Anthology*, May 2022

"Light" (print), "Present", "Gnat Creek", Changing Names" and "Pear Blossom" (online reprints) - *California Quarterly* Vol 48 No.1 2022

"Study of Blood's Limits" – *Peculiar: A Queer Literary Journal,* Summer 2022

"Cholera Season" – Alternating Current Press, *The Coil Literary Magazine,* 2022

"Tide Riddle" and "Dandelion Coffee" - *Hedge Apple,* June 2022

"Chainsaw Haiku" (2022) and "Peach Season" (2023) - *Twelve Mile Review*

"Cholera Season" – *Poet's Choice,* Monsoon Anthology, 2022

"Do Stones Have Souls?", "Fig", "All Poems Are Moon Poems", "Rings", "Lunar New Year", "Rainbows Dreaming" (print), "Light" "Gnat Creek", "Honey", "Present", "Pear Blossom" (reprints) - *California Quarterly,* Crystal Fire Anthology October 2022

www.ingramcontent.com/pod-product-compliance
Lightning Source LLC
Chambersburg PA
CBHW022103020426
42335CB00012B/804